18 UNKNOWN SUTRAS

YOU MUST KNOW BEFORE BUYING YOUR

DREAM HOME

18 UNKNOWN SUTRAS YOU MUST KNOW BEFORE BUYING YOUR DREAM HOME

Yashaswi Shroff

Worldwide Published by

Pendown Press

PENDOWN PRESS LLP

An ISO 9001 & ISO 14001 Certified Co.,

Regd. Office: 3767A, Kanhaiya Nagar,

Tri Nagar, Delhi-110035

Ph.: 8130886000, 9650072927, 8595249536

E-mail: info@pendownpress.com

Branch Office: 1A/2A, 20, Hari Sadan, Ansari Road,

Daryaganj, New Delhi-110002

Ph.: 011-45794768

Website: PendownPress.com

First Edition: 2024

Price: ₹399/-

ISBN: 978-93-5554-900-6

Layout and Cover Designed by Pendown Graphics Team
Printed and Bound in India by Thomson Press India Ltd.

।। जय श्री गणेश ।।

Dedication

This book is a tribute—a tribute to the journey every home buyer in India embarks upon, the journey of making the most significant financial decision of their lifetime. It's dedicated to you, the reader, who stands on the precipice of transforming a dream into a tangible reality. Through the pages of "18 Unknown Sutras You Must Know Before Buying Your Dream Home," may you navigate this journey "haule haule," with wisdom, insight, and foresight. It's a call to spread this knowledge far and wide, embracing the power of informed decisions and becoming a beacon for others in the vast sea of home buying.

With deep gratitude, this book also pays homage to the architects of my life—my mentors, gurus, and the lineage of strength and vision that has shaped me. To my revered grandparents and parents, whose stories of resilience and innovation light my path; to my in-laws, for their relentless support and belief in me; to my sisters and brothers-in-law, for being the pillars of encouragement and love.

A special dedication to my wife, Aakriti, who is the essence of strength, grace, and unwavering support. Her journey alongside me, especially through the transformative experiences of pregnancy and the birth of our daughter

Tanaira, has been a testament to her incredible fortitude and love. Aakriti, you have been my rock, inspiring me to be the best version of myself every day, crafting this book amidst life's profound changes and challenges.

And to my greatest gift, my daughter Tanaira, who embodies the future and the reason for striving towards creating a better world. This book is for you and because of you.

"18 Unknown Sutras You Must Know Before Buying Your Dream Home" is more than just a guide; it is a dedication to the collective journey of making informed and heartfelt decisions in creating the spaces we call home. To all who walk this path, may you find clarity, confidence, and joy in the choices you make, building not just homes, but legacies.

Contents

Preface

In the vast tapestry of life, few decisions hold as much weight and importance as buying a home. It's not just a financial transaction; it's a deeply emotional journey towards establishing a haven for ourselves and our loved ones. Understanding the gravity of this decision, and the myriad challenges and uncertainties that accompany it, I felt compelled to pen down "18 Unknown Sutras You Must Know Before Buying Your Dream Home."

This book originates from my own experiences, woven into the fabric of resilience, foresight, and integrity passed down through generations. Having been at the crossroads of numerous real estate endeavors, I've witnessed firsthand the complexities and nuances of this industry. Yet, what struck me most profoundly was the recurring narrative of homebuyers navigating their path with a mixture of hope and uncertainty, armed with dreams but often lacking the guidance they need.

This book is my endeavor to bridge that gap, to transform uncertainty into confidence, and to illuminate the path with the lantern of awareness and understanding. It's a distillation of years of experiences, lessons learned not just

from successes but, more importantly, from the hurdles and setbacks that have been invaluable teachers.

Homebuyer's Power Manual is structured around the concept of Sutras—principles that are simple yet profound, designed to enlighten and guide. Each chapter, or Sutra, delves into a critical aspect of the home buying process, from understanding the legalities and financial planning to appreciating the nuances of property appreciation and community living. It's a holistic guide intended to empower you, the reader, to make decisions that resonate with your dreams, aspirations, and realities.

Beyond the practical insights, this book is a narrative of hope, a testament to the belief that with the right knowledge and guidance, the journey to owning your dream home can be a fulfilling and joyful experience. It's an invitation to join me in a mission to elevate the discourse around real estate, to move beyond transactions to build lasting relationships and communities where dreams flourish and legacies are built.

As you turn these pages, I hope you find not just answers but inspiration, not just guidance but a partner in your journey. This book is a reflection of my personal mission to add value to the lives of homebuyers, to be a growth partner who stands by you as you navigate one of the most significant milestones of your life.

Welcome to "18 Unknown Sutras You Must Know Before Buying Your Dream Home." Here begins your journey toward making an informed, confident, and heartening decision in creating your home—a journey I am privileged to share with you.

Yashaswi Shroff

Foreword

Yashaswi, along with his senior family members, has always supported me in designing their developments at Alcove as "communities," which will always lead to success as the residents enjoy their homes and a lifestyle with like-minded individuals.

In this book, he has taken an extremely bold move to educate and simplify the complex process of home buying. It is a must-read guide to navigate the maze of home-buying and ease one through one of the biggest decisions in life. Its simple layout will guide you through the much-needed information covering all aspects of finding and purchasing your house.

My best wishes to Yashaswi for this book, and the Alcove family for developing Happy Communities and satisfying customers.

Ar. Hafeez Contractor

Leading Real Estate Architect of India

Padma Bhushan Awardee

Foreword

I read this book & found it to be so practical & simple for any layman to understand... a must read for anyone planning to buy their dream home. Each sutra of this will make your buying decision with 100% certainty. I felt astonished as to why no developer educates their buyer before selling... great job Yashaswi!!

Rajesh Mittal

Chairman & MD

Greenply

Foreword

In our sacred Indian spiritual and cultural tradition, known as Sanatana Dharma or Bharatiya Sanskriti, everything is sacred. Every moment of our lives presents an opportunity to fulfill our dharma through our karma (actions) andget closer to the true purpose of life: God Realisation or Self-Realisation. We don't confine spirituality to just what happens in temples. Instead, we think it's part of everything we do - every breath we take, every choice we make. Buying a home fits into this picture too.

In life's journey, the aspiration for a home often becomes a significant milestone. It signifies more than just needing a place to live; it reflects our deep desires for security, peace, and a sense of belonging. "18 Sutras You Need to Know Before Buying Your Dream Home" explores this journey deeply. It blends practical and spiritual aspects, helping you make choices that truly match who you are.

A home is more than a shelter; it is a sanctuary that should mirror the tranquility, spaciousness, and light of your inner being. This book delves into the essence of creating a space that not only serves your physical needs but also nurtures your spirit.

The 18 sutras shared here are like precious pearls of wisdom, encouraging you to think deeply about what truly matters, guiding you to see past the surface attraction of material things to discover what brings true happiness and peace in your life.

In a world where success is often measured by how much we gather, these sutras bring back the focus to mindfulness, gratitude, and living in harmony with nature. They prompt us to think about our impact on the environment, the vibes in our spaces, and the kind of community we surround ourselves with. Each sutra acts as a gentle nudge toward mindful living, urging us to fill our homes with love, light, and positive vibes.

May your home be a reflection of your journey, filled with peace, love, and the divine light that resides within us all.

And, of course, to live on the banks of Mother Ganga is one of the greatest blessings we can ever hope for, as it is a place filled not only with grace, shakti, and blessings, but as we watch Mother Ganga flow, we tap into the eternal, divine, sacred flow of the Mother Goddess within ourselves.

With love and peace from the holy banks of Mother Ganga,

In Sacred Service,

Sadhvi Bhagawati Saraswatiji

International Director, Parmarth Niketan Ashram, Rishikesh

Author of #1 Best-seller "Hollywood to the Himalayas: A Journey Of Healing & Transformation"

About the Author

Yashaswi Shroff, the visionary Marketing Director of Alcove Realty, stands out for his pivotal role in conceptualizing and executing 'THE 42,' Kolkata's tallest and most luxurious residential tower. A graduate of St. Xavier's College, Kolkata, Yashaswi's journey in real estate was enriched by invaluable experiences at Ernst & Young, shaping his unique perspective on the industry.

His professional journey is characterized by a profound dedication to the real estate sector, highlighted by his innovative leadership and strategic execution in various residential projects. Further affirming his position as an industry leader, Yashaswi has been honored with numerous prestigious awards for his exceptional contributions to the luxury real estate sector, including:

➢ 'Realty+ 40 Under 40' award in 2022.

➢ 'Young Achiever of the Year' at The Economic Times Real Estate Conclave Awards (East) in 2022.

Throughout his illustrious career, Yashaswi has held several key positions, bringing transformative ideas to the forefront of the industry:

➢ National Committee Head, New Construction Technology, CREDAI Youth Wing (2020-2022)

➢ East Zone Coordinator, CREDAI Youth Wing (2023-present)

➢ Member of the Senior Managing Committee, CREDAI Bengal (2023-present)

➢ Founding Member & Chair, PHDCCI West Bengal Chapter

Beyond his professional endeavors, Yashaswi is an avid wildlife enthusiast and golfer, blending his love for nature and sport with his business acumen.

As an author, Yashaswi embarks on a new journey with his debut book, "18 Unknown Sutras Before Buying a New Home." This book encapsulates his cumulative experience of 100 years in the Home Buying Industry, aiming to demystify the home-buying process for new buyers. As India's First 'Home-Buying Scientist,' he combines technical know-how with a deep understanding of buyers' aspirations, making his insights invaluable for anyone embarking on the journey of acquiring their dream home.

Yashaswi's engagement extends beyond business; he is deeply committed to understanding the dreams and needs of prospective homeowners. This empathetic and hands-on approach has not only defined his professional success but also positions him as a trusted guide in the complex world of real estate.

Yashaswi Shroff

India's 1st Home Buying Scientist

Marketing Director, Alcove Realty | Author

About The Book

In the dynamic world of real estate, the relationship between homebuyers and builders often navigates through a landscape of skepticism and trust. Common perceptions have painted builders in a less favorable light, characterized by delays in delivery, unfulfilled promises, and a perceived disconnect between what's committed and what's delivered. **"18 Unknown Sutras You Must Know Before Buying Your Dream Home"** aims to bridge this divide, offering a fresh perspective on the builder-homebuyer relationship. Here's how this book stands as a beacon of change for the average Indian homebuyer:

From a Limited Viewpoint to an Expanded Understanding:

Before: Many homebuyers enter the market with a narrow viewpoint, often influenced by common misconceptions about builders—believing that delays and unfulfilled promises are the norms.

After: Readers will gain a panoramic understanding of the real estate process, equipped with the knowledge to navigate the market with confidence and clarity.

Transforming Skepticism into Trust:

Before: Initial doubts about builders' commitment to timely delivery and honesty in keeping their word.

After: Insight into the builder's perspective, underscoring a mutual commitment to creating happy communities, thereby fostering a foundation of trust.

Decoding the Real Estate Process:

Before: The complexities of buying a home can seem daunting due to a lack of clear, accessible information.

After: The book breaks down the home buying process into digestible sutras, empowering homebuyers with the knowledge to make informed decisions.

Personal Journey to Professional Insights:

Before: Homebuyers often feel they are navigating the purchasing process alone.

After: Yashaswi Shroff shares personal stories and professional victories, offering readers a mentor who understands their journey on a personal level.

Shifting from Transactional to Transformational Relationships:

Before: The builder-homebuyer relationship is viewed as purely transactional.

After: Readers will see the potential for relationships built on mutual respect, understanding, and shared goals for community happiness and individual satisfaction.

Bridging the Knowledge Gap:

Before: There's a common belief that insightful secrets of home buying are reserved for the few.

After: The book shares these 'secrets' openly, ensuring every reader is as well-informed as the most seasoned property investor.

"18 Unknown Sutras You Must Know Before Buying Your Dream Home" is not just a typical guide. It's a journey of enlightenment that reshapes how the average Indian homebuyer approaches the task of finding their dream home. Through detailed insights, real-life examples, and a commitment to transparency, Yashaswi Shroff invites readers to move beyond traditional methods and feel more confident about buying a home. This book is a companion for anyone ready to expand their horizons, understand the depth of real estate intricacies, and ultimately, make choices that lead not just to the purchase of property but to the foundation of a home filled with joy and free of regret. Welcome to a transformative experience that will not only change how you view real estate but also redefine your role within it.

Chapter-1

Deep Dive into the Problem

My Grandfather, Sri Amar Nath Shroff, was born in Parbatipur, a small town in Bangladesh (formerly East Pakistan), in the year 1941. My family was involved in many businesses at the time, which were set up by our ancestors. Fortunately, my great-grandfather had the vision of having a second base so that the family could relocate overnight in case of any disturbances in their locality. He began setting up the second base in Deogarh, formerly Bihar and now Jharkhand.

The Pillar of Deogarh

During that time, East Pakistan saw domestic violence and a lot of disturbances, due to which my great-grandfather made the decision to relocate his family to Deogarh, where he had already built a house. This was the first major transformation in my family, which was only possible due to the foresight of my great-grandfather. He soon made his mark in Deogarh as the 'nagar seth' and was involved in the business of purchasing and selling food grains. One of the popular markets in Deogarh also became known as

'Laxmi Bazaar', named after my widely respected great-grandmother. This market still exists and continues to be known by the same name.

A New Horizon: The Kolkata Chronicles

After graduating from Patna Law College, my grandfather felt compelled to escape the dominance of his great-grandfather's personality. He decided to move to Kolkata in the year 1961 along with his wife and newborn son, giving up all his well-established legacy and with a fire in his belly to make a name for himself, all on his own. With only a few rupees in his pocket and no place to call home, he embarked on a journey to build his own reputation. Despite the initial challenges, he found his footing as a lawyer in the Calcutta High Court, working with M/s B.M. Bagaria & Co. Under Mr. B.M. Bagaria's guidance, he honed his legal skills and developed a unique approach to his work, setting himself apart in the industry.

From Legal Expertise to Real Estate Visionary

After practicing law for a few years, driven by ambition, he realized real estate held the key to achieving big goals with limited resources. He made a bold switch to real estate, and this was the second biggest monumental moment for him and his family, shaping their future and starting a new legacy. He laid the foundation of Alcove Realty from a 100 sq. ft office with just 4 staff in Lal Bazaar, he tackled his first project on Salimpur road in 1981. His legal background proved helpful, yet he encountered unexpected hurdles, learning the complexities of the industry firsthand.

During this journey, he learned a lot from tackling tough projects, but more so from 11, Diamond Harbour Road, which subsequently changed to 14/2 Burdwan Road (Siddhartha Building). Here, 70 Cottahs of land were sold to us, but subsequently, it transpired that 45 Cottahs of land had been declared as "Excess Vacant Land" and surrendered by the landowner to the Land Ceiling Department. It was really a painful venture and a learning opportunity to rectify the land and make it a successfully completed venture.

Diamond City South was another painful purchase as out of about 600 Cottahs, there was land under about 250 Cottahs. Furthermore, it was occupied by such dangerous gangsters that it was very difficult to get it vacated. Thirdly, it was affected by the provisions of land ceiling. It took a lot of time, energy, and money to overcome all these difficulties. It was truly satisfying to overcome these obstacles, and we finally completed this project successfully.

There are many other projects where he faced numerous unique challenges, but he overcame them through his grit, determination, and hard work, ultimately achieving success.

He immersed himself in every aspect of the real estate business, from small details to major endeavors, always embracing challenges with a thirst for learning. Overcoming setbacks including planning issues, local authority approvals, and managing various obstacles, he continually refined his approach, discovering better methods along the way. Even today, his expertise is sought after for navigating challenging situations. Recognizing the value of continual learning and innovation, he absorbed knowledge on the job and through interactions within the industry, pioneering groundbreaking projects and concepts in Eastern India. Notably, he developed Kolkata's first condominium project, 'Brindavan Gardens,' in 1990, and introduced amenities such as a health club, beauty parlour, and swimming pool in the early 90s with Siddhartha Building in Alipore, showcasing his innovative mindset and commitment to progress.

Upholding the Legacy: The Next Generations

Since my grandfather lived and worked on his own terms and had a very dominating personality, he thought it was best for my father to also work in a similar fashion. Hence, he encouraged my father to go through the grind himself and create an independent legacy. As a result, my father started working in the garments industry, associating with Siyarams, where he developed strong skills in garments and fabrics. On another note, this still helps me as I only trust him for the selection of all my formal wear and the stitching of my suits, shirts, and trousers. He then moved on to the infrastructure business in the year 1993, primarily engaging in highways and flyovers construction. He played a part in the construction of projects such as the Mumbai-Pune Expressway and Jalandhar bypass.

Even though we come from a traditional Marwari family, my grandfather encouraged my mother, who got married at the age of 16, to join the business and be an active working member of the family. This was another milestone moment for us, as my mother joined the business and started managing the finances and accounts of our company, assisting both my grandfather and father. Today, she continues to head our finance and accounts team and has a team of Chartered Accountants working under her, despite her education being limited to Class 10.

From Setbacks to Success: The Rise of Diamond Days

The late 90s and early 2000s were financially very difficult for my family, as real estate was also not doing good and my father struggled to make ends meet during his time working on the Jalandhar Road construction project. The year 2003 was the darkest time for our family, as my parents had to literally run away from Jalandhar overnight, despite the project being 98% complete, budgeting issues and cash flow problems led to this drastic decision. My father had no funds left to pay off the creditors, and my grandfather, burdened by debts from the failing real estate business, could offer little support. However, all of their intentions were good, and their hearts were in the right place. They never wanted to cheat anyone or withhold repayment of debt money to the lenders. Unfortunately, our family's net worth was deeply negative, amounting to crores, with no incoming funds.

I strongly believe that God always does what is best for us, as long as we continue to work hard and honestly. This pivotal moment brought our family together in Calcutta to face the crisis and start anew. At the age of 12, I witnessed some of the hardships my family endured. My parents, my two elder sisters, and I used to share a room to save on electricity costs. Our landline phones used to constantly buzz, and I remember one night when my eldest sister received a call from a creditor who was very agitated, demanding repayment of his money. I remember growing up with a fleet of drivers and cars at home, but we had to sell off most of our cars and let go of the drivers as we could not afford them anymore. My mother used to drive all her children to tuition classes and for other house errands.

Despite these challenges, my grandfather and father maintained composure, dealing with creditors daily while assuring them of repayment when circumstances improved. Alongside my mother, they sought solutions to overcome this adversity. It was during this time that Mr. Shyam Sundar Agarwal emerged as an angel for our family. Despite society's skepticism and lenders' doubts, Mr. Agarwal believed in our integrity and vision. In 2004, my grandfather, along with Mr. Agarwal and two other partners, founded "Diamond Group," embarking on a new journey.

Through grit, determination, faith, the relentless support of our new partners, and a lot of hard work, we were able to launch remarkable projects such as Diamond Chambers, Diamond City West, Diamond City North, and Diamond City South, which completely turned us around within a matter of a couple of years. The first thing that my family did with the new cash flow into the system was to repay all the old creditors and remove the past liabilities. I remember how a few people completely changed their attitude towards us. Just a while ago, they would be threatening and demeaning my family and had lost their hopes of ever getting their money back. But, when they received a call from our end and without any follow-up, they got their money back which by then would have been bookedas bad debt by them; they were astonished and pleasantly surprised.

I saw a live example in my teenage years of how manifestation and hard work could do wonders. From a point where we were almost about to sell off our home and shift to a very small rented home to the point where we were able to rebuild ourselves completely, it was unbelievable. Due to strong manifestation, we got the support of macro-economic conditions also favoring us in that situation when India saw its golden boom period between 2004-2008, which fueled our bounce back and growth.

During this period, property prices appreciated manifold, which no one could have predicted in such a short while. Additionally, the overall buying power of people increased due to many job creations and stock market boom. We got very secure financially, and my grandfather always had great ambitions to rise higher and continue to make a mark by doing remarkable, innovative and iconic projects. His ambition was not just driven by the desire to make money, but rather by the aspiration to embark on unique, groundbreaking endeavors that would create a legacy and name worth far more than anything else.

From Boarding School to Business

I went to an international boarding school in Bangalore for my +2 from 2007-2009. Despite 98% of my classmates choosing to study abroad for their undergraduate studies, I decided to return to Kolkata with the ambition of joining my family business. Observing my mother over the years, I realized the importance of being your own "munim" in the business. Therefore, I decided to pursue C.A. back in Kolkata alongside my college studies. I enrolled in the B.Com (Hons) program at St. Xavier's College, Kolkata, attending morning sessions from 6 AM to 10 AM. For my CA Articleship, I joined Ernst & Young to gain work experience. While many students from business families would opt for a dummy experience certificate, I chose to actively work and gain experience outside of my own organization. This decision proved invaluable as it exposed me to different industries and businesses, without anyone treating me as someone from a privileged background. I worked at the ground level and assisted in internal audits and the preparation of SOPs for various businesses during my stint at EY.

I successfully passed the 1st and 2nd level examinations of CA on my first attempt and continuously enhanced my academic skills across all subjects in the business and accounting field through classroom learning and various tuition sessions. My college life was devoid of typical experiences as I remained occupied throughout the day, either working or studying, which helped me evolve as a person and learn the art of discipline and focus. I faced failure at the CA final exam level three times, which was a big setback as I was always brilliant academically and had never seen failures. I understood the real meaning of why wise people say that it is important to face failures in life, as the amount of learnings that you gain from failures is much greater than all your success stories. I had already extracted all the academic and practical knowledge while pursuing CA and decided not to invest any more time in trying to qualify as a CA. This was a very hard decision for me, since I had worked very hard to earn this degree for 5 years. But I got a call from the universe to let go of the degree and instead join my family business, which had always been my goal since the time I passed out of school.

My Foray into the Family Legacy

In January 2016, I officially joined Alcove Realty and spent my initial months shadowing my grandfather. During this time, I learned invaluable lessons in discipline, relationship-building, delegation, talent extraction, humility, hard work, and customer interaction. These experiences deeply influenced my approach to business and instilled values such as "Under commit - Over Deliver" into our company culture.

I got a fantastic opportunity a few months down the road - 'The 42'. I got a chance to lead the project and oversee the day-to-day operations across all the functions. Through all the support, guidance and learnings from my grandfather, father, and other project partners, I successfully completed what became the most iconic project in Eastern India. Upon its completion, 'The 42' became the highest occupied building in India. Even though my grandfather is usually not a very expressive person, he told me how satisfied he was to see me grow and cross all the hurdles and challenges that came my way during the course of this project. It was the most satisfying moment of my life. The discussions I used to have with him were adding to my growth exponentially, as he told me that I was seeing things and facing situations in my late 20s, which he was also experiencing for the first time close to his 80s. And then he suggested envisioning the impact of experiencing events like these at this stage of my career, highlighting the profound and immense learning opportunities they would offer on my journey.

While I was busy working on constructing, marketing, selling, and delivering 'The 42' wholeheartedly, a wonderful opportunity came our way in 2017 in the form of a huge land parcel of approximately 29 acres in Serampore on the banks of the Ganges. We had almost acquired this piece of land in 2012 and had already completed the planning of a mega township project, but at the last minute, the land acquisition deal did not go through. Over the next 4-5 years, this land was shown to all the developers in Kolkata, yet no one dared to acquire it in an area like Serampore, fearing the risk of low sales velocity far away from the main city by developing such a mega project. The Almighty helped us to finally acquire this land in 2017, and since all our planning to develop this project was ready, we just took a few months to get the plans sanctioned and obtain all necessary approvals and launched this project on 11th February, 2018. We saw it as a golden opportunity by connecting all the 3 sub-plots within the land through an underpass with G.T. Road on one side and the Ganges on the other. We took up the project as a challenge to do something remarkable and iconic within the affordable housing segment following our DNA of continuous innovation and value addition to our customers. Approximately 60 lakh sq. ft. project by itself Alcove New Kolkata pushed us to bring a fresh way of working, and we did many firsts of its kind in the industry:

➢ Alcove New Kolkata became the first platinum-rated green building in the affordable housing sector in India, driven by our value of developing environment friendly green buildings.

➢ It became the first, finest, and grandest township with High-rise residential towers in the affordable segment on the banks of the Ganges in West Bengal.

➢ It became the first project to have a private Ganga ghat, jetty, and ferry service on the river.

➢ We became the first developer in East India and among the very few all India to set up an in-house aluminum window factory.

➢ We also became the first developer in East India to have our own fire door factory.

➢ Alcove New Kolkata Prayag - the first residential phase of this project with 6 High-rise towers of G+30 storeys (approximately 15 lakh sq. ft.), was completed and delivered within about 3.5 years, almost 1.5 years before our committed timeline despite facing COVID disruption of 2 years. After the first lockdown in 2020, we were the first project in West Bengal to resume our construction activities by taking all safety protocols.

➤ Alcove New Kolkata Prayag was nationally recognized by the Central Government as the "Best Affordable EWS/LIG Housing Project in West Bengal" at the PMAY (Pradhan Mantri Awas Yojana) - Empowering India Awards 2022.

Since the completion of 'The 42', I have been deeply involved in transforming my company. Recognizing the need for alignment between our culture to our growth trajectory, as well as our future plans, I realized that the strategies that propelled us from 0 to 100 in the last four decades wouldn't suffice to propel us from 100 to 1000 in the next decade. That's when I started working on shifting the company culture to make it more system-oriented and less dependent on individuals. Along with my entire team, I came up with a new cultural statement: "Together We Can". I also realised the importance of shifting from a sales-oriented company to a "marketing-oriented, sales-driven" company. I diligently started implementing the most valuable lesson from my grandfather, emphasizing the importance of staying directly connected with customers.

Over the last few years, I have invested 100s of hours in communicating with customers at each stage of the buyer's journey. I remember feeling apprehensive and fearful before embarking on this journey of direct interaction with customers. I worried about how I would effectively communicate and connect with them, as well as how I would handle their problems and queries. However, I soon realised that starting anything new is always difficult at the start, but it becomes easier over time. I left everything to the Almighty and trusted in the path that he showed me.

Today, if someone were to wake me up at 3 A.M. to connect with a customer, I am confident in my ability to do so easily, without any doubt.

Mission Empowerment:
Educating Homebuers -

I conducted a research study during my journey and realised that 83% of the home buyers were not even aware of the critical parameters they should consider before making the most important financial decision of buying a home for themselves. Consequently, they would often make mistakes, and most home buyers would feel cheated or experience regret later for not making the correct decision. The feeling of being cheated would come either because the promises made by the builder were not fulfilled or because they had certain assumptions or perceptions in their head without knowing all the facts themselves.

This is when I decided that now my life's mission is to educate all the home buyers in India - no matter where they want to buy their dream home or what their budget is, about some of the unknown sutras that they must know before they make that all-important financial decision of buying a new dream home.

My purpose and Alcove Realty's purpose were strengthened when I interacted with so many buyers. I realised that we are not merely in the business of acquiring land and selling real estate; rather, we are in the business of making happy communities that last forever, even after we handover the project. Therefore, each project we undertake and every minute we invest in our work is all driven by this purpose.

Chapter-2

Unveiling the Craftsmen of Your Dream Home

Introduction to a Home Buyer's Journey

When you set your heart on buying your dream home, you're not just investing money; you're entrusting your dreams and future to the hands that build it. The first step in this journey, "Know the Real Minds Behind the Project," is about understanding the people whose expertise and integrity shape your future abode. It's crucial to look beyond the walls and the paint to see the vision and values of those who lay the foundation and bring the structure to life.

The Team Crafting Your Future

A real estate project is like a large canvas painted by various artists. Each stroke is guided by professionals dedicated to turning a vision into reality. These include not just the builder but also architects, MEP (Mechanical, Electrical, Plumbing) consultants, structural consultants, green building consultants, environmental consultants, soil consultants, landscape consultants, and clubhouse interior designers. Their collective expertise ensures your home is not only a place of comfort but a sanctuary of safety, efficiency, and beauty.

Builder: The Visionary Leader

The builder or developer is at the heart of your home's creation. Their mission, vision, and team strength are your first indicators of their capability to fulfill your dream. Recognition and awards highlight their commitment to excellence, but it's their track record of promises kept, areas developed, and adherence to quality that truly tells their story. This narrative is not about buildings but about building communities where dreams thrive.

Consultants: The Pillars of Excellence

➢ Architects design your home with an eye for beauty and functionality, ensuring spaces that breathe and inspire.

➢ MEP Consultants weave the essential services into the fabric of your home, making it a model of comfort and convenience.

➢ Structural Consultants ensure the building stands strong against the tests of time and nature, safeguarding your sanctuary.

➢ Green Building Consultants champion sustainability, making your home a friend to the environment.

> Environmental and Soil Consultants validate the health of the land and its surroundings, ensuring a safe foundation for your dreams.

> Landscape Consultants craft the green spaces that envelop your home in nature, enhancing its beauty and tranquility.

> Clubhouse Interior Designers imagine and realize the communal spaces where memories and friendships blossom.

Beyond Material Gains: The Real Mission

The true mission that drives these professionals goes beyond material gains. It's about creating spaces that nurture, inspire, and stand the test of time. It's about innovation, sustainability, and community. As a buyer, researching these motivations can offer deep insights into the project's potential to meet your dreams. Explore their portfolios, read interviews, and attend project launches to hear directly from the minds behind the project.

Empowering Questions for the Buyer

Equipping yourself with the right questions can transform your home buying journey. Ask the builder:

> What is the vision and mission driving this project?

> Can you share the track record and achievements of your team and consultants?

➢ How do you ensure the sustainability and environmental friendliness of your projects?

➢ What innovations have your projects brought to the real estate sector?

The Power of Public Platforms

Remember, transparency is your ally. Platforms like RERA (Real Estate Regulatory Authority) provide invaluable data on projects across India, including legal approvals, project status, and builder credibility. Utilize these resources to make an informed decision, ensuring your dream home becomes a reality.

Conclusion

Understanding the real minds behind your dream project is crucial. It's about connecting your vision with those who have the passion, integrity, and expertise to bring it to life. This first sutra sets the foundation for a home buying journey that is not only informed but deeply personal, paving the way for the enlightening principles that follow.

Chapter-3

Deciphering the Hidden Charges in Your Home Purchase

The Joyous Path to Homeownership and Its Financial Twists

Embarking on the journey to owning your dream home is an exhilarating adventure, filled with hopes and aspirations. However, this path is also intertwined with financial intricacies that, if overlooked, can turn your dream into an unexpected financial ordeal. The second sutra, "Know Your Project's Hidden Charges," aims to shine a light on the less discussed yet significant financial aspects of buying a home, ensuring your journey remains both joyous and financially sound.

Understanding the Landscape of Hidden Charges

The price tag of your dream home is often just the tip of the iceberg. Below the surface, a myriad of additional charges lurks, which can substantially inflate the final cost. These charges come in various forms and titles, each with its implications on your financial planning. Here's a closer look at some of these charges commonly employed by developers in India:

➢ **Extra Development Charges (EDC):** Levied for infrastructure developments like roads, sewage, and utilities.

➢ **Preferential Location Charges (PLC):** Imposed for homes in more desirable locations within a project, such as those facing parks or waterfronts.

➢ **Floor Escalation Charges (FEC):** Applied for properties on higher floors, often justified by promising better views or reduced noise.

➢ **Clubhouse Membership and Maintenance Deposits:** Upfront charges access to clubhouse facilities and future maintenance services.

➢ **Legal and Documentation Fees:** Costs associated with legal formalities and documentation processes.

The Critical Role of GST in Your Financial Planning

GST (Goods and Services Tax) plays a pivotal role in the financial equation of buying a new home. The applicable GST rate is determined by the sales value of the property, with different slabs in place (typically 1% or 5%). It's crucial to note that these rates are subject to change based on government policies. For instance, properties below a certain value might attract a lower GST rate, aimed at making affordable housing more accessible. Given these dynamics, it's essential to inquire about the current GST regime applicable to your purchase and remain informed about any government announcements that might affect these rates.

Stamp Duty and Government Incentives

Stamp duty is a state-specific charge and plays a significant role in the overall cost of acquiring a property. Post-COVID, several state governments, including West Bengal, have announced stamp duty rebates to stimulate the real estate market. These incentives can offer significant savings and often come with a limited timeframe. Being informed about such rebates and integrating them into your financial planning can improve the affordability of your dream home.

Empowering Questions for the Buyer

To navigate through the financial complexities of home buying, arm yourself with questions that demand transparency and clarity:

➢ Can you provide a comprehensive breakdown of all costs associated with this purchase, including but not limited to EDC, PLC, FEC, and any legal fees?

➢ What is the current GST rate applicable to this property, and how does it affect the total cost?

➢ Are there any ongoing government incentives, such as stamp duty rebates, that I should be aware of?

➢ How do these additional charges compare to those of other projects in the area?

➢ In case I decide to cancel my flat, what would be the cancellation charges, and how long will it take to receive a refund of my balance money?

Conclusion

The dream of homeownership should not be clouded by unforeseen financial burdens. By understanding the multitude of hidden charges and asking the right questions, you can ensure a transparent and informed purchase process. This sutra equips you with the knowledge to uncover and address these hidden charges, paving the way for a financially secure and joyous home buying experience.

Chapter-4

Embracing the Heart of Your Dream Home: The Community

Beyond Bricks and Mortar:
Embracing the Essence of Community

The journey towards finding your dream home often navigates through the features and facilities of the property, focusing on tangible aspects like layout, room sizes, and amenities. Yet, nestled within the heart of this decision is an element that transcends the physicality of the home - the community. Sutra 3, "Know Your Project's Community," delves into the invaluable aspect of the people and the environment that envelopes your potential home, advocating for a holistic view of community living.

The Resident's Community:
A Tapestry of Lives

The fabric of a project's community is woven from the diverse threads of its residents. Understanding who your neighbors will be is not just about ensuring social compatibility; it's about envisioning a future where your life is enriched by those around you. For families with children, the community offers a vital cultural and social fabric that supports high ambitions and shared values. Children find friends and mentors outside school, within a setting that reinforces the values cherished by their families.

For those considering a serene abode for retirement or planning ahead for their parents, the demographic composition holds the key to a lively and supportive elderly community. A neighborhood that fosters inclusivity and activity for senior residents ensures that the golden years are filled with joy, companionship, and a profound sense of belonging.

The Surrounding Ecosystem: Essential Services and Social Infrastructure

The community's value is also significantly enhanced by the basic and emergency necessities available in its vicinity. Proximity to grocery stores, medical care facilities, pharmacies, diagnostic centers, and educational institutions adds layers of convenience and peace of mind to daily living. Additionally, amenities for celebrations and leisure, such as hotels, banquet halls, temples, beauty parlors, cinemas, and shopping centers, enrich the social fabric, making the community not just a place to live but a space to thrive.

The Art of Community Research

Understanding the project's community requires a blend of research and interaction:

➢ **Engage with the Builder:** Inquire about the demographic profile of buyers and the envisioned community lifestyle within the community. Builders often organize meet-and-greet events for potential and existing buyers, providing a glimpse into the community dynamics.

➢ **Visit the Site:** Experience the vibe of the surrounding area. Observe the available facilities and amenities and assess how they align with your lifestyle needs.

➢ **Connect with Future Neighbors:** Social media platforms and community forums can offer insights into the resident community. Engaging in conversations can provide a real sense of the community spirit and values.

Empowering Questions for the Buyer

To integrate your life story into the fabric of a new community, consider these questions:

➢ Can you describe the demographic profile of the residents buying into this project?

➢ How does the project cater to families with children, in terms of cultural and social environments?

➢ What amenities are conveniently located nearby for essential services, leisure, and social engagements?

> Are there community groups or forums where potential buyers can interact with existing or future residents?

Conclusion

A home is more than a space; it's a community that nurtures and inspires. "Know Your Project's Community" encourages you to look beyond the physical attributes and understand the essence of community living. This sutra guides you to choose a home that doesn't just meet your physical needs but also enriches your life with meaningful connections and a supportive environment.

Chapter-5

Crafting Foundations:
The Blueprint of Excellence

Unraveling the Design Philosophy

At the heart of every great real estate project lies a profound design philosophy, a blueprint that guides every decision, from the drawing board to the final brick. This sutra delves into the essence of understanding a project's design philosophy, highlighting its importance in aligning with the expectations and aspirations of the home buyer.

The design philosophy encapsulates the vision of the architect, builder, and their panel of consultants, meticulously crafted through deep market research and collaborative innovation. It reflects the intended character of the project, its environmental harmony, and how it promises to enhance the lives of its residents. For a home buyer, grasping this philosophy offers insights into the project's soul, ensuring it resonates with their lifestyle and values.

Adopting Modern Construction Technologies

The evolution of construction technology has brought about revolutionary methods like aluminum shuttering, replacing traditional brickwork with precision and efficiency. This advancement not only accelerates the construction process but also ensures a higher quality of structural integrity. For a home buyer, understanding whether a project utilizes such cutting-edge technologies is crucial. It speaks volumes about the builder's commitment to quality and innovation. Further, exploring whether the builder has implemented backward integration, such as establishing their own factories for aluminum windows or fire doors, can offer assurances of quality control and timely completion.

Assurance Through Quality Control

The integrity of a building is the sum of its parts— each material and equipment piece plays a pivotal role in its longevity. A discerning home buyer should delve into the builder's quality management process for materials and the rigorous quality control (QC) measures applied during construction and finishing phases. Issues like dampness in walls plague many homes across India, making it imperative to inquire about the builder's damp prevention strategies and accountability measures post-possession.

Aesthetic and Finishing:
A Reflection of True Quality

The aesthetic appeal and finishing touches of a project are not merely about visual pleasure but are indicators of the quality and durability of materials used. Home buyers should seek detailed information about the brands of bathroom fittings, door locks, paints, putty, and flooring materials. This knowledge can prevent future dissatisfaction and ensure that the home remains a source of pride and joy long after possession.

Green Building Certification:
A Commitment to the Environment

In an era where environmental sustainability is no longer a choice but a necessity, understanding a project's green building initiatives is paramount. Home buyers, especially in pollution-affected cities like Delhi and Kolkata, should prioritize projects with green building certifications from recognized authorities like IGBC or GRIHA. These certifications are not just badges of honor; they represent a builder's commitment to reducing the environmental footprint and enhancing the health and well-being of its residents.

Empowering Questions for the Buyer

To navigate the multifaceted landscape of real estate, equip yourself with questions that illuminate the path:

➢ Can you share the design philosophy of this project and how it aligns with modern living standards?

➢ What construction technologies have been adopted to ensure quality and efficiency?

➢ How does the builder manage the quality of materials, and what QC measures are in place during construction?

➢ Could you provide details regarding the brands and specifications of the materials used in the project's aesthetics and finishing?

➢ Is this project recognized with any green building certifications, and what sustainable practices have been integrated?

Conclusion

Understanding the foundational elements that constitute your potential home—from its design philosophy to its commitment to quality and sustainability—offers a comprehensive view of what to expect from your investment. This sutra guides you through the critical aspects of project evaluation, ensuring your decision is informed, your investment is sound, and your future home is a testament to excellence.

Chapter-6

Foundations of Safety: Building Trust and Peace of Mind

The Ethos of Construction Safety

Embarking on the journey of creating a home extends beyond architectural designs and material selections; it is deeply rooted in the practices and principles upheld during its construction. Sutra 5, "Know Your Safety," unfolds into two critical dimensions, starting with the ethical and karmic considerations of construction safety. The safety protocols and practices adopted by a builder not just safeguard the lives of laborers but also imbue the project with a spirit of care and respect.

As believers in the law of karma, understanding the builder's commitment to construction safety becomes a matter of conscience for potential homeowners. It's about ensuring that the foundation of your future home is not marred by negligence or harm. This emotional and ethical inquiry into the builder's safety practices reveals a deeper understanding of the values that will permeate your future home, fostering a space that is not only physically secure but also spiritually serene.

Ensuring a Secure Environment for Residents

The second dimension of safety transcends the construction phase, focusing on the long-term security and well-being of the residents. A thorough exploration of the security measures in place is essential for ensuring that your future home is a bastion of safety for your family. While CCTV systems have become a staple in modern residential projects, their implementation details, such as coverage areas (including elevators) and data retention duration, are crucial aspects that demand scrutiny.

Moreover, the approach to managing and monitoring access into the community holds paramount importance. Inquiring about the use of advanced systems like MyGate for visitor management can provide insights into the project's commitment to leveraging technology for enhanced security. Additionally, the presence of Automatic Rescue Devices (ARD) in elevators is a testament to thoughtful safety measures, ensuring that residents are not left vulnerable during power outages.

Empowering Questions for the Buyer

To navigate the critical aspect of safety within your potential home, arm yourself with questions that shed light on both construction practices and residential security:

➢ Can you provide details about the safety protocols followed during the construction phase to protect the workers?

➢ Can you elaborate on the labour welfare programs such as health camps and eye check-up camps?

➢ How does the project ensure the long-term safety and security of its residents?

➢ What measures, including technological solutions, are in place for access control and visitor management within the community?

➢ Can you provide details on the emergency systems, such as ARD in elevators, to safeguard residents during power outages?

Conclusion

"Safety," in its deepest essence, encompasses both the ethical practices during construction and the measures implemented to secure the well-being of residents. This sutra invites potential homeowners to delve into the ethos of safety that shapes their future home, ensuring it is a place of trust, peace, and spiritual harmony. By prioritizing safety from an informed perspective, you lay the foundation for a home that is not only a physical sanctuary but also a testament to care, respect, and responsibility.

Chapter-7

Sustaining Brilliance:
The Art of Maintenance

Moving Beyond Possession:
Preparing for Ongoing Care

As we journey further into the realm of informed home buying, Sutra 6, "Know Your Project's Maintenance," illuminates an often-overlooked yet fundamental aspect of homeownership—the transition from construction to maintenance. This transition signifies more than just receiving keys; it marks a critical phase that shapes the long-term health and vibrancy of your community. Understanding the nuances of maintenance, from the selection of the Facility Management (FM) Agency to the establishment of a reserve sinking fund, is pivotal for ensuring that the project's brilliance is preserved through the years.

The Role of Facility Management (FM) Agency

The choice of an FM Agency and the timing of its onboarding are crucial decisions that significantly impact the project's maintenance quality. A proactive approach, where the builder is involved in selecting and onboarding the FM Agency months before project completion, ensures a seamless transition of knowledge. This includes preventive maintenance schedules, warranties, and Annual Maintenance Contracts (AMCs). Such foresight facilitates a comprehensive handover, embedding maintenance practices that resonate with the builder's original vision of excellence.

The Significance of Early FM Agency Engagement

Late appointment of the FM Agency often leads to a fragmented transition, where critical information and best practices are lost in translation. This oversight can result in inadequate maintenance, escalating costs, and diminished property value. Home buyers, therefore, should inquire about the builder's strategy for FM Agency selection and involvement, emphasizing the importance of early engagement for effective knowledge transfer and maintenance planning.

The Reserve Sinking Fund:
A Financial Safeguard

Another pivotal aspect of maintenance is the establishment of a reserve sinking fund. This fund serves as a financial cushion for major repairs or renovations, ensuring that the property remains in optimal condition without imposing unexpected financial burdens on the residents. Enquiring about the formation, management, and utilization policies of the reserve sinking fund offers insights into the project's commitment to sustainability and long-term care.

Empowering Questions for the Buyer

To navigate the complexities of project maintenance, arm yourself with questions that uncover the commitment to sustaining the property's value and quality:

➢ How does the builder support the selection and onboarding of the FM Agency, and at what stage is this process initiated?

➢ What measures are in place to ensure a comprehensive transition of maintenance knowledge and practices to the FM Agency?

➢ Can you explain the policies and practices surrounding the establishment and management of a reserve sinking fund?

Conclusion

The journey of owning a home extends far beyond its construction and possession; it evolves through the meticulous care and maintenance that follows. "Know Your Project's Maintenance" sutra beckons home buyers to look into the future, ensuring that the property they choose is supported by a solid foundation of maintenance practices.

This foresight not only safeguards the physical integrity of the home but also preserves its essence, ensuring that if the builder's vision was to create a diamond, it remains a diamond, sparkling through the decades.

Chapter-8

Navigating Amenities and Environment: A Balance of Needs and Nature

Crafting Spaces That Resonate: Understanding Amenities

In today's evolving residential landscape, amenities have become a cornerstone of marketing strategies, enticing buyers with the promise of a luxurious and convenient lifestyle. However, Sutra 7 encourages homebuyers to transcend the allure of quantity and delve into the quality and relevance of these facilities. "Navigating Amenities and Environment: A Balance of Needs and Nature" underscores the importance of aligning amenities with the specific needs and desires of your family, ensuring they enrich your life in meaningful ways.

Selecting a home encompasses more than just counting amenities; it's about the compatibility of these features with your lifestyle. For instance, the inclusion of hobby rooms, music rooms equipped with instruments, and gaming cafes can significantly enhance the quality of life for children and teenagers, providing spaces for joy and creativity without disrupting the tranquility of home. Likewise, the design and material of walking or jogging tracks, and the selection of equipment in the gym, speak volumes about the thoughtfulness placed in the well-being of residents.

Moreover, for families with pets, the presence of pet-friendly amenities such as exclusive pet parks and dedicated zones for pets to play and relieve themselves is invaluable. These considerations not only cater to the needs of pet owners but also maintain harmony within the community by respecting the preferences of all residents.

Embracing the Environment: Beyond Your Home's Borders

The ambiance of your future home extends beyond its immediate boundaries to encompass the surrounding environment. The quality of air (AQI), sound pollution levels during festive and election times, and water quality are pivotal factors that impact daily living and well-being. Homebuyers should seek comprehensive information about these aspects, understanding how developers are addressing environmental challenges within the project's design and infrastructure.

For instance, initiatives to mitigate sound pollution, water purification systems, and green spaces designed to enhance air quality reflect a project's commitment to offering a healthy living environment. These elements are especially crucial in urban settings, where the bustle of city life can often encroach upon the peace and tranquility of residential areas.

Empowering Questions for the Buyer

To ensure that the amenities and environmental considerations align with your needs and values, consider these questions:

- ➢ How do the amenities provided cater to the specific needs of my family, including children, seniors, and pets?
- ➢ Can you provide details about the quality and specifications of amenities, such as gym equipment and communal area materials?
- ➢ How much open area do you have?
- ➢ How have the open areas been utilized?
- ➢ What measures have been implemented to address environmental concerns, particularly regarding air and water quality within the project?
- ➢ How does the project mitigate sound pollution, especially during festive times or late-night/early morning hours?

Conclusion

Choosing a home that harmonizes with your lifestyle and values requires a careful assessment of both the amenities provided and the environmental attributes of the project. "Navigating Amenities and Environment" guides you through this process, emphasizing the importance of quality, relevance, and sustainability. By focusing on what truly matters to you and your family, you can find a home that not only meets your desires but also contributes to your well-being and happiness.

Elevating Expectations: The Dynamics of Vertical Commutation

Ascending to New Heights: Understanding Lift Systems

In the towering aspirations of high-rise living, the efficiency and reliability of vertical commutation systems become fundamental to the daily comfort and convenience of residents. Sutra 8, "Elevating Expectations: The Dynamics of Vertical Commutation," encourages homebuyers to delve into the specifics of lift systems, often overlooked amid the appeal of architectural aesthetics and amenity offerings. This chapter underlines the importance of evaluating the brand, service support, speed, and capacity of lifts as integral to the decision-making process.

The choice of lifts in a residential project speaks volumes about the developer's commitment to quality and resident satisfaction. Reputable brands with proven track records in preventive and breakdown maintenance ensure that the vertical journey within your home is both smooth and secure. Beyond the brand, the technical specifications, such as lift speed and the number of lifts per tower, directly impact the daily routine of residents, influencing wait times and overall accessibility.

Navigating Peak Hours and Emergency Scenarios

One of the most revealing aspects of a high-rise's lift system is its performance during peak hours. Prospective homeowners should inquire about the anticipated average and maximum waiting times after calling a lift, especially during busy morning and evening hours. These details are not just about convenience but also about planning for efficient time management.

Moreover, the availability of stretcher lifts is a critical consideration, showcasing the project's readiness for health emergencies. The ability to accommodate a stretcher in a lift is not only a marker of thoughtful design but also an essential feature that could potentially save lives, ensuring that every second counts during critical moments.

Empowering Questions for the Buyer

In the pursuit of a home that rises above the ordinary, arm yourself with questions that illuminate the efficacy of its vertical commutation system:

> Can you specify the brand of lifts used in the project and their reputation for reliability and service support?

> What are the technical specifications of the lifts, including their speed and the number of lifts available in each tower?

> During peak hours, what are the expected average and maximum wait times for a lift?

> Is a stretcher lift included in the project's design to facilitate emergencies?

Conclusion

The intricacies of vertical commutation in high-rise living are a testament to a project's foresight and dedication to resident well-being. "Elevating Expectations" guides homebuyers through the critical evaluation of lift systems, ensuring that the journey to your home in the sky is not only seamless but also safe and accommodating. By prioritizing these considerations, you can assure that your choice of residence stands tall not only in stature but in satisfaction and safety as well.

Chapter-10

Harmonizing Spaces:
The Essence of Energy and
Design in Your Home

Cultivating Positive Energy:
The Role of Natural Ventilation and Vastu

In the quest of a home that not only provides shelter but also nurtures its inhabitants, Sutra 9, "Harmonizing Spaces: The Essence of Energy and Design in Your Home," guides homebuyers through the nuances of creating a living space infused with positive energy. This chapter delves into the critical aspects of natural ventilation, the strategic use of vastu principles, and the profound impact they have on the well-being of residents.

The flow of natural light and air plays a pivotal role in enhancing the energy level within a home. Large windows in all rooms, including kitchens and toilets, ensure that every corner of your abode is kissed by sunlight and breezed by fresh air, fostering a vibrant and healthy living environment. Beyond the physical benefits, the alignment with vastu principles further amplifies the home's positive energy. Adherence to vastu can influence the layout of the project and individual flats, guiding the placement of rooms in a manner that enhances wealth, health, and happiness. For instance, ensuring the entrance of the house is positioned in a vastu-compliant direction can attract prosperity, while the kitchen's placement in the southeast corner is believed to promote good health.

Celebrating Nature's Ballet: Views and Balconies

The magic of witnessing a sunrise or sunset, and the serene beauty of a full moon night from the comfort of your home, brings a unique sense of joy and peace to everyday life. The orientation of your flat and its windows can dramatically influence your ability to enjoy these natural spectacles, making it essential to consider these aspects when selecting your future home.

Balconies serve as private havens that extend your living space into the outdoors, offering a breath of fresh air amidst urban living. The size, layout, and absence of service lines running through balcony walls enhance its utility and aesthetic appeal. Tailoring the balcony space to fit your lifestyle, whether for morning yoga sessions, a cozy reading nook, or a vibrant space for plants, adds a personalized touch to your home.

Framing Your World:
The Impact of Views

The vista from your windows frames your daily perspective, influencing your mood and outlook. Whether it's the dynamic energy of a city urban view, the calming presence of a garden, the tranquility of a water body, or the privacy offered by strategically placed landscapes, the type of view matters significantly. This chapter encourages homebuyers to prioritize what views align with their desires and how these perspectives contribute to the overall ambiance and energy of the home.

Empowering Questions for the Buyer

In your search for a home that resonates with positive energy and harmony, consider these guiding questions:

➢ How does the project and flat design incorporate natural ventilation and sunlight in alignment with vastu principles?

➢ Are there specific features or orientations within the flat that enhance the enjoyment of natural phenomena like sunrises, sunsets, or the full moon?

➢ What considerations have been made regarding the size and layout of balconies, and are there any obstructions to their full utilization?

> ➤ What types of views are available from the flat, and how do they align with my personal preferences and lifestyle needs?

Conclusion

"**Harmonizing Spaces**" invites homebuyers to explore the deeper aspects of home selection, emphasizing the importance of energy, design, and nature's interplay. By prioritizing these elements, you ensure that your home is not just a place of residence but a sanctuary of well-being, harmony, and joy. This chapter serves as a compass, guiding you towards making informed decisions that align with your innermost desires for a home that truly feels like your own.

Chapter-11

The Comparative Project Checklist: Simplifying Your Home Buying Journey

Unraveling the Complexities of Home Buying with a Universal Approach

The journey to finding your dream home is a path filled with aspirations, decisions, and at times, overwhelming choices. "The Comparative Project Checklist: Simplifying Your Home Buying Journey," Sutra 10, introduces a vital navigational tool for homebuyers across India, incorporating practical examples with a touch of West Bengal's essence. This chapter presents a strategy designed to transcend regional boundaries, offering practical examples infused with the essence of West Bengal, yet applicable universally.

The Challenge Without a Checklist

Consider the story of Arjun and Mousumi, who are on a quest to find their dream home in the heart of Kolkata. Overwhelmed by the plethora of options and seduced by compelling sales pitches, they navigate their search without a structured approach. Their decision, influenced by the allure of numerous amenities, leads to a purchase that falls short of meeting their daily needs and long-term happiness. This scenario highlights the challenge of navigating through an abundance of unstructured information, often leading to confusion and regrettable, delayed decisions.

The Clarity Brought by a Comparative Project Checklist

In contrast, Rahul and Priya, equipped with a Comparative Project Checklist (CPC), embark on their search with clarity and focus. They prioritize factors such as natural light, accessibility to workplaces in Bengaluru, and a supportive community for their growing family. Their checklist enables a systematic comparison across their shortlisted projects, guiding them to a decision that is not only timely but perfectly aligned with their needs. This approach not only saves them from potential price hikes but also secures a home that is a true reflection of their aspirations.

Implementing the CPC: A Strategy for All

The Comparative Project Checklist becomes a beacon for buyers, illuminating the path through the dense market. For instance, a checklist might reveal:

➢ Project G offers luxurious amenities but lacks in Vastu compliance, pushing the budget boundaries.

➢ Project H aligns with Vastu and fits the budget but offers limited amenities.

➢ Project I strikes a balance with adequate amenities, Vastu features, and a reasonable price, albeit in a less preferred location.

Tailoring Questions for Informed Decisions

Leveraging the CPC effectively means asking the right questions:

➢ How do my 'must-have' features compare across the shortlisted projects?

➢ Which project aligns best with my long-term lifestyle goals and aspirations?

➢ What compromises am I willing to make, and how do they stack up against each option on my checklist?

➢ Based on the checklist, which project emerges as the closest match to my ideal home?

Conclusion

The tales of Arjun and Mousumi versus Rahul and Priya illustrate the transformative power of the Comparative Project Checklist in the home-buying process. This strategic tool not only addresses the issue of analysis paralysis but also ensures decisions are made with clarity, efficiency, and a deep sense of personal fulfillment. By adopting a structured, data-driven approach, homebuyers are empowered to navigate the complex landscape with confidence, making choices that resonate with their dreams and realities.vastu principles, and the profound impact they have on the well-being of residents.

Chapter-12

Banking on Trust: The Significance of Project Approvals by Financial Institutions

Elevating Your Assurance:
The Role of Bank Approvals in Home Buying

In the complex process of home buying, one critical aspect often overlooked by buyers is the examination of the project's approval status by various banks for home loans. "Banking on Trust: The Significance of Project Approvals by Financial Institutions," Sutra 11, shines a light on this pivotal checkpoint, emphasizing its importance regardless of whether the purchase is financed through savings or loans. This chapter endeavors to underscore how the backing of a project by reputable and conservative financial institutions, such as the State Bank of India (SBI), serves as a symbol of reliability and adherence to regulations, offering homebuyers an added layer of security and confidence.

The Litmus Test of Legitimacy

Consider the scenario where a project is endorsed by a multitude of banks, including some of the nation's most conservative and diligent financial institutions.

This endorsement is not merely a formality but a testament to the project's adherence to legal and regulatory compliances. Banks conduct a thorough due diligence process, evaluating the project's legal standing, developer's credibility, and the overall feasibility before granting their approval for home loans. For a homebuyer, this serves as a litmus test of the project's legitimacy and financial viability.

Interpreting Bank Approvals: A Buyer's Perspective

Imagine Kaushik and Puja, who are in the process of selecting their dream home. They come across two projects: Project J, approved by multiple banks including SBI, and Project K, with limited financial endorsements. Kaushik and Puja recognize that the broad spectrum of approvals for Project J implies a thorough validation of its credentials, significantly reducing their risk as potential homeowners. This understanding propels them towards making an informed decision, favoring a project that not only meets their aesthetic and functional needs but also stands tall on the grounds of financial and legal scrutiny.

The Assurance Beyond the Surface

When a project receives approval from esteemed banks, it signifies more than just financial stability; it indicates a level of trust in the project's completion and delivery timelines, the quality of construction, and adherence to legal regulations. This assurance is invaluable for homebuyers, offering peace of mind and a safeguard against potential legal or financial hurdles in the future.

Empowering Questions for the Informed Buyer

To leverage the security offered by bank approvals, prospective buyers should consider the following questions:

➢ Which banks have sanctioned home loans for this project, and what does this indicate about the project's compliance and credibility?

➢ How do the number and reputation of these banks align with my risk assessment and confidence in the project?

➢ What due diligence processes do these banks undertake before granting their approval, and how can this information guide my decision-making?

➢ Beyond the financial aspect, what does the project's approval by conservative banks say about its overall quality and reliability?

Conclusion

Understanding the significance of a project's approval status by financial institutions is akin to building your home on a foundation of trust and assurance. "Banking on Trust" empowers homebuyers with the knowledge to discern the credibility and stability of their potential home, ensuring their investment is secure and their future is built on solid ground. This chapter, through practical examples, illustrates the profound impact of bank approvals on the home buying process, advocating for a decision that is well-informed, confident, and free of regret.

Chapter-13

Navigating the Maze of Parking Solutions in Your Dream Project

The Unseen Importance of Parking Decisions

In the blueprint of your dream home, parking may seem like a footnote compared to architectural aesthetics and amenities. Yet, as "Navigating the Maze of Parking Solutions in Your Dream Project," Sutra 12 illustrates, the type, location, and additional features of parking facilities can significantly impact daily convenience and future readiness. This chapter aims to guide homebuyers through the often-overlooked complexities of parking solutions, ensuring their choice enhances the overall living experience.

Exploring the Range of Parking Alternatives

Parking solutions within a residential project can vary widely, from open-air spots to sophisticated mechanized systems that maximize space. Each type comes with its nuances:

➢ **Open Parking:** These are uncovered spaces within the project premises, often the most economical option.

> **Covered and Basement Parking:** Offer protection from weather, with basement parking providing additional security but requiring navigation through ramps.

> **Mechanical and Stacked Parking:** Innovative solutions for space constraints, though they may involve higher maintenance.

> **Dependent vs. Independent Parking:** Dependent parking spaces cost less but may require moving other vehicles to access yours, while independent parking offers direct access at a premium.

> **Exclusive Parking:** Specially designated spots, possibly with EV charging facilities, cater to the growing trend of electric vehicles.

The Evolving Needs: EV Charging and More

As electric vehicles (EVs) increasingly become part of our daily lives, the readiness of your new home's parking facilities for this transition becomes crucial. Inquiring about EV charging stations within the project becomes a forward-thinking move, aligning with the inevitable shift towards greener transportation.

The Case of Adequate Parking

Often, homebuyers underestimate their current and future parking needs, leading to challenges down the line. The story of Neha, who purchased an additional parking spot in anticipation of her family's second car, underscores the foresight needed. Unlike scenarios where residents scramble for visitor parking during gatherings, Neha's proactive decision to invest in ample parking space pays off, offering convenience and flexibility. Furthermore, while visitor parking typically isn't purchased individually, it remains a critical amenity that projects usually accommodate to ensure guest comfort.

The Overlooked Aspect: Vehicle Care Services

An often overlooked aspect in the home-buying process is the availability of vehicle care services within the project. Regular maintenance facilities like car wash stations and water outlets can significantly contribute to the maintenance and longevity of your vehicle. Imagine leaving your car in a well-maintained project with regular car cleaning services versus finding it covered in dust and bird droppings after a long absence. The difference in care can keep your vehicle in excellent condition, echoing the project's commitment to not just resident but also vehicle well-being.

Empowering Questions for the Buyer

To navigate the parking maze effectively, equip yourself with these queries:

➢ What types of parking are available, and how do they align with my current and future vehicle needs?

➢ Are there plans for installing EV charging stations, and how does the project intend to expand these facilities?

➢ How does the project accommodate visitor parking, ensuring convenience for guests?

➢ What vehicle care services are offered within the project to maintain my car in top condition?

Conclusion

Parking is not just about securing a spot for your vehicle; it's about ensuring ease, security, and future-readiness in your residential choice. By giving due consideration to the types of parking and associated amenities, you make a decision that adds daily convenience and long-term value to your dream home. "Navigating the Maze of Parking Solutions" equips you with the knowledge to prioritize parking in your home-buying decision, ensuring your choice is comprehensive and future-proof.

Chapter-14

Crafting Your Nest:
Bridging the Gap Between
Possession and Perfection

The Final Mile in Home Creation

The journey to turning a newly acquired space into a home is a path filled with decisions, desires, and often, daunting challenges. "Crafting Your Nest: Bridging the Gap Between Possession and Perfection," Sutra 13, delves into an essential yet frequently overlooked aspect of home buying—the transition from basic construction to personalized living space. This chapter aims to illuminate the crucial phase of interior finishing and furnishing, a task that traditionally demands a significant investment of time, money, and energy from the homebuyer.

Decoding the Standard Finish of Indian Homes

In India, a new home typically comes with basic finishes that include flooring, kitchen counters, sinks, toilets, wall tiles, bathroom fittings, doors, windows, and electrical fixtures. However, the canvas of a home extends far beyond these elements, requiring the homeowner to undertake the challenging task of furnishing and designing the space to reflect personal taste and functionality.

The Traditional Route vs. Developer Assisted Fitouts

Traditionally, homeowners like Soumitra and Rina would navigate through numerous stores, juggle consultations with interior designers, and meticulously select furniture, appliances, and décor to piece together their dream home. This process, fraught with budget miscalculations and time constraints, often leaves many overwhelmed and their homes incomplete.

On the other hand, consider Anirban and Mousumi, who opted for a project where the developer offered add-on fit-out services and assistance in interior finishing. The developer provided a comprehensive checklist of items needed to complete their home, along with contacts for preferred vendors who offered special prices negotiated for the project's homeowners. This structured approach not only streamlined the furnishing process but also ensured cost-effectiveness and a cohesive design aesthetic.

The Importance of Developer Tie-Ups and Assistance

The advantage of having developer-assisted fit-outs or tie-ups with interior service providers cannot be overstated. Such collaborations can notably ease the burden on homeowners by offering:

➤ **A Streamlined Process:** Reducing the need to visit multiple stores or coordinate with various service providers.

➤ **Cost Savings:** Leveraging bulk purchasing and negotiated deals that benefit all homeowners within the project.

➤ **Design Cohesion:** Maintaining a consistent design theme that aligns with the overall aesthetic of the residential project.

➤ **Time Efficiency:** Minimizing the time gap between possession and moving in, making the transition smoother and faster.

Empowering Questions for the Homebuyer

To navigate this crucial phase effectively, prospective buyers should inquire about the following:

➤ Does the developer offer any interior finishing or furnishing services post-possession?

➤ Can you provide a list of recommended vendors or service providers for interior fit-outs?

> ➤ Are there negotiated deals or discounts available for homeowners within this project for furnishings and appliances?

> ➤ How have other homeowners in this project approached the task of completing their homes, and what services were most beneficial?

Conclusion

The transition from a structurally complete space to a fully realized home is a journey of personal expression and practicality. "Crafting Your Nest" guides homebuyers through understanding the pivotal role developers can play in easing this transition. By choosing projects that offer or assist with interior finishing services, homeowners can significantly reduce the stress and uncertainty traditionally associated with this phase, ensuring their dream home is realized with joy, not trepidation.

Chapter-15

Financial Foundations for Your Dream Home: A Guide to Smart Planning

Setting a Financial Roadmap

Embarking on the journey to purchase your dream home involves more than just selecting the perfect location or amenities; it requires meticulous financial planning. "Financial Foundations for Your Dream Home: A Guide to Smart Planning," Sutra 14, aims to demystify the financial aspects of home buying, offering insights into traditional and transformative strategies for managing finances, including leveraging tax exemptions, understanding home loan nuances, and recognizing the significance of your CIBIL score.

Maximizing Tax Benefits: Navigating Income Tax Exemptions

In India, the Income Tax Act provides several avenues for homebuyers to alleviate their financial burden through exemptions and deductions. Specifically, under Section 54, homebuyers can claim exemptions on capital gains from the sale of a property, provided the gains are reinvested into purchasing or constructing a new home. This exemption can significantly reduce the taxable income, potentially saving lakhs in taxes, depending on the capital gains incurred.

Additionally, Section 80C allows for deductions on the principal repayment of a home loan up to INR 1.5 lakhs annually, while Section 24(b) offers deductions on interest payments up to INR 2 lakhs annually. Together, these deductions can lead to substantial yearly savings, easing the financial load of acquiring a new home.

Consider two scenarios: Arjun, who takes advantage of both Sections 54 and 80C, effectively reduces his taxable income by INR 3.5 lakhs annually, translating to significant tax savings. In contrast, Nikhil, unaware of these provisions, misses out on these benefits, paying a higher tax without need.

The Crucial Role of Home Loans: Understanding Eligibility and Costs

For many, home loans are the bridge to achieving their dream of homeownership, offering favorable interest rates and flexible repayment options. Understanding loan tenure, EMI affordability, the impact of your CIBIL score, hidden charges and eligibility criteria is crucial.

Take, for example, Sunita, a young IT professional in Bengaluru, who assesses her financial stability and opts for a 20-year home loan, balancing her EMI commitments with her monthly income. Her journey highlights the importance of aligning loan terms with personal financial health to ensure a stress-free path to homeownership.

A high CIBIL score, reflecting responsible credit behavior, not only enhances your loan eligibility but can also secure you a more favorable interest rate. Conversely, a low score may result in higher rates or even loan rejection.

Boosting Your CIBIL Score: Practical Tips

Maintaining a high CIBIL score is pivotal. Regularly monitoring your credit report, timely repayment of existing loans, and maintaining a healthy credit utilization ratio are key strategies. For instance, Sunita, with a high CIBIL score of 750, secures a home loan at an attractive interest rate, while Rahul, with a score of 600, faces higher rates and limited loan options.

Unveiling Hidden Charges and the Power of Developer Tie-Ups

Awareness of potential hidden charges, such as processing fees or foreclosure charges, is essential. Developers who have tie-ups with banks can often negotiate waivers or reductions of these fees, offering an added advantage to buyers.

Empowering Questions for Financial Readiness

To navigate your financial planning effectively, consider:

- ➢ How can I maximize my tax benefits under Sections 54, 80C, and 24(b) when purchasing my home?

- ➢ Based on my age, income and savings, what home loan tenure and EMI structure best suit my financial plan?

- ➢ Based on my income and CIBIL score, what are my eligibility and expected interest rates for a home loan?

- ➢ What steps can I take to improve my CIBIL score ahead of applying for a loan?

- ➢ Are there developer-bank tie-ups that can offer me reduced processing fees or other financial benefits?

Conclusion

"Financial Foundations for Your Dream Home" equips you with the knowledge to navigate the financial aspects of home buying with confidence. By understanding and leveraging tax benefits, optimizing your CIBIL score, and being aware of the nuances of home loans, you can lay a solid financial foundation for acquiring your dream home, ensuring a process that is as rewarding financially as it is personally.

Chapter-16

Empowering Homebuyers: Navigating Through RERA

Unveiling the Shield of RERA

In the evolving landscape of the Indian real estate sector, the Real Estate (Regulation and Development) Act, known as RERA, stands as a bastion of protection for homebuyers. Sutra 15, is designed to illuminate the path for individuals venturing into the property market, equipping them with knowledge about their rights and the recourse available under RERA. As an expert RERA consultant, this chapter aims to demystify the Act, showcasing how it can be a powerful ally in ensuring fair play and transparency in real estate transactions.

The Core of RERA:
Safeguarding Homebuyer Rights

At its core, RERA is about safeguarding the interests of homebuyers by ensuring accountability and transparency from developers. Key provisions include:

- ➤ **Timely Delivery:** RERA mandates that developers complete and hand over properties within the agreed timeline, failing which, they are liable to compensate the buyer.

- ➤ **Accurate Representation:** All advertisements and project details must accurately reflect the final product. Any deviation allows the buyer to seek redress.

- ➤ **Advance Payment:** Developers can only ask for up to 10% of the property's cost as an advance before signing a sale agreement, protecting buyers from hefty upfront charges.

Real-life RERA Success Stories

Consider the case of Aditi and Rohan, who faced delays in the possession of their new apartment in Mumbai. Armed with knowledge about RERA, they filed a complaint against the developer for the delay. The RERA authority intervened, ensuring not only that they received their apartment but also compensation for the delay.

In another instance, Priya discovered post-purchase that the amenities promised by the developer were not provided. Utilizing RERA's provisions, she was able to hold the developer accountable, resulting in the amenities being installed or receiving adequate compensation.

Navigating Grievance Redressal with West Bengal RERA

The RERA grievance redressal mechanism is a cornerstone of its protective framework, offering a direct channel for resolving disputes. For instance, in West Bengal, homebuyers can file a complaint with the West Bengal Housing Industry Regulation Authority (WBRERA), detailing any promises unfulfilled by the developer.

Take the case of Ananya, a resident of Kolkata, who found discrepancies in the clubhouse facilities upon possession. By filing a complaint with WBRERA, Ananya initiated a process that not only ensured the developer adhered to the promised standards but also highlighted the effectiveness of RERA in upholding buyer rights.

Tips for Harnessing the Power of RERA

To fully leverage RERA for a secure home buying experience, consider the following tips:

➢ **RERA Registration:** Always ensure that the project is RERA registered. This registration number is a testament to the project's legitimacy.

➢ **Project Details:** Utilize the RERA portal to access detailed project information, including approvals, land status, and track record of the developer.

➤ **Grievance Redressal:** Familiarize yourself with the process of filing complaints under RERA for prompt resolution of disputes.

Empowering Questions for the Vigilant Homebuyer

Before diving into your home buying journey, arm yourself with these essential inquiries:

➤ Is the project and developer duly registered under RERA, and what is the registration number?

➤ Am I able to review the comprehensive project plan, including timelines and amenities, as filed under RERA?

➤ How does the RERA grievance redressal mechanism work, and what steps should I follow if my rights are violated?

Conclusion

Navigating through RERA empowers homebuyers with a formidable toolset to protect their interests in the real estate market. By understanding and utilizing the provisions and protections offered under RERA, buyers can confidently step into property transactions, assured of fairness, transparency, and recourse in the face of discrepancies. "Empowering Homebuyers: Navigating Through RERA" serves as a guide to harnessing these protections, ensuring a safe and informed home buying process.

○　○　○　○

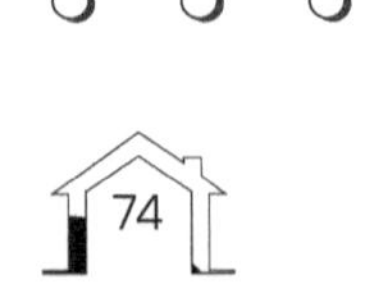

Chapter-17

Securing Future Prosperity: Strategic Insights on Property Appreciation

The Art of Future-Proofing Your Home Investment

Embarking on the journey of homeownership extends beyond mere possession; it's a long-term investment potentially ripe with financial rewards. "Securing Future Prosperity: Strategic Insights on Property Appreciation," Sutra 16, is meticulously crafted to guide homebuyers through the intricacies of ensuring their investment flourishes over time. Focusing on the broader picture, including the sustainable growth of the community and meticulous property maintenance, this chapter aims to illuminate the path to maximizing the future value of your home, whether through appreciation or rental yields.

Looking Beyond the Purchase: Sustaining Your Investment

Consider the narrative of the Das family from Kolkata, who recognized the value of investing in a project known for its diligent maintenance and strong community bonds. Over two decades, their property's value significantly surpassed the average market rate, a testament to the importance of selecting a project with a long-term vision for growth and upkeep. This example underscores the vital consideration that the future appreciation of a property is intricately linked to the ongoing care and vibrancy of its environment.

The Untapped Potential of Rental Yields

Transforming a property into a rental asset offers a tangible avenue for generating passive income. The Majumdar family illustrates this potential by leasing their strategically located apartment to expatriates. The key factors that elevated their property's rental appeal included modern amenities, proximity to international schools and business hubs, and access to green spaces. Such attributes not only enhance the living experience but also position the property as a desirable rental option, ensuring a steady income stream.

Adding Value for Tomorrow: Practical Strategies

For homeowners aspiring to safeguard and enhance their property's future worth, consider:

➢ **Proactive Maintenance:** Regularly upgrading and maintaining your property can significantly boost its market and rental appeal.

➢ **Community Engagement:** Active participation in community welfare and decision-making processes fosters a cohesive and attractive living environment, thereby contributing to overall property value.

➢ **Market Awareness:** Keeping abreast of real estate developments and trends in your area can offer insights into optimal times for selling or renting out your property.

Strategic Planning for Future Selling or Renting

Preparing for the future sale or rental of your property requires foresight and strategic planning:

➢ **Documentation and Compliance:** Ensure all property documents are in order and comply with local regulations to facilitate a smooth transaction.

➢ **Marketing Your Property:** Effectively showcasing your property's unique features, such as sustainability initiatives or bespoke designs, can attract premium buyers or tenants.

➢ **Adapting to Market Needs:** Understanding the evolving preferences of homebuyers and tenants allows you to make targeted improvements that increase your property's desirability.

Empowering Questions for the Forward-Thinking Homebuyer

To navigate the future financial landscape of your property effectively, deliberate on:

➢ How does the project's vision align with future market trends and community growth?

➢ What amenities and features of the property are most likely to appeal to future buyers or tenants?

➢ How proactive steps can I take to enhance my property's value through maintenance and upgrades?

➢ What are the current and emerging factors influencing rental yields and property appreciation in my area?

Conclusion

"Securing Future Prosperity" offers a comprehensive guide for homebuyers to not only secure a home that meets their present needs but also ensures it stands as a testament to wise investment for the future. By embedding strategic considerations for property appreciation and rental potential from the outset, homebuyers can pave the way for financial security and growth, making their home a cornerstone of their investment portfolio.

Chapter-18

Beyond the Sale: Navigating Post-Sales CRM Services

Elevating the Home Buying Experience with CRM

The conclusion of a sales agreement often marks the beginning of a waiting period filled with anticipation and, sometimes, uncertainty for many homebuyers. "Beyond the Sale: Navigating Post-Sales CRM Services," Sutra 17, seeks to illuminate the critical aspect of customer relationship management (CRM) post-sale, an area where expectations can diverge significantly from reality. This chapter aims to educate homebuyers on the services and support they should anticipate and demand from developers after the initial transaction, ensuring a transparent and informed journey to homeownership.

The Digital Bridge: Online Customer Portals

In today's digital age, staying informed about the progress of your future home should be straightforward and accessible. Developers who offer online customer portals provide homebuyers with a valuable tool, enabling them to view construction updates, access critical documents, and track milestones from the comfort of their homes. For instance, consider the experience of the Banerjee family, who could monitor the development of their Kolkata residence through such a portal, alleviating concerns and fostering a sense of involvement in the construction process.

Personalized Support: The Role of a SPOC in CRM

The provision of a Single Point of Contact (SPOC) within the developer's CRM team can significantly enhance the homebuyer's experience. This dedicated representative serves as a liaison, addressing queries, providing updates, and ensuring a personalized and seamless communication flow. The Ghosh family, for example, benefited greatly from their SPOC's regular updates and assistance, making their home-buying journey smoother and more transparent.

Keeping Homebuyers in the Loop: Regular Construction Updates

Understanding the progress of your future home is paramount. Developers committed to transparency should provide regular construction updates through emails, newsletters, or the customer portal. These updates allow homebuyers like Mr. and Mrs. Das to remain connected to the evolution of their investment, even when site visits are impractical due to safety or logistical reasons.

The Handover Takeover (HOTO) Mechanism: Ensuring a Smooth Transition

The possession stage is a pivotal moment for homebuyers, marking the transition from anticipation to reality. A structured Handover Takeover (HOTO) process goes beyond the mere exchange of keys; it involves a comprehensive orientation about the property, including demonstrations of home features, warranty documentation for fittings and appliances, and guidance on maintenance practices. The Sharma family's positive experience, where the developer conducted a detailed HOTO process including a walkthrough of the apartment's features and a review of warranties and maintenance tips, exemplifies a best practice in customer service.

Empowering Questions for Future Homeowners

To ensure a fulfilling post-sales experience, prospective homebuyers should consider asking:

➢ Does the developer provide an online customer portal for construction updates and document access?

➢ Will I have a designated Single Point of Contact for queries and updates throughout the construction phase?

➢ What is the frequency and mode of construction updates, and how can I access them?

➤ Can you describe the HOTO process in detail, including any orientation or training provided about the apartment's features and maintenance?

Conclusion

The journey to homeownership is enriched by developers who value and invest in robust post-sales CRM services. "Beyond the Sale" underscores the importance of clear, consistent communication and personalized support, guiding homebuyers to set their expectations and demand a level of service that matches the significance of their investment. By advocating for transparency, engagement, and education throughout the post-sale phase, homebuyers can navigate this period with confidence and clarity.

Cultivating Serenity:
The Essence of Landscaping
in Your Community

The Green Canvas of Home

Among the myriad factors that enhance the appeal of a residential project, landscaping often shines subtly yet significantly. "Cultivating Serenity: The Essence of Landscaping in Your Community," Sutra 18, invites homebuyers to delve deeper into the verdant aspects of their potential homes, moving beyond the percentages of open area to the soulful integration of hardscape and softscape. This chapter aims to enlighten homebuyers, including those in vibrant Bengali communities, on the profound impact of thoughtful landscaping on the well-being and aesthetic harmony of their living spaces.

The Symphony of Hardscape and Softscape

Landscaping is an art that blends the structural beauty of hardscaping with the natural elegance of softscaping. Take, for example, the story of the Banerjee family, who chose their home in a Kolkata suburb, enticed by the project's promise to lush gardens and well-designed walkways. The project's thoughtful selection of native plants, tranquil water bodies, and shaded seating areas created an oasis that elevated their daily living experience, emphasizing the importance of both hardscape and softscape in crafting livable, inspiring environments.

The Language of Flora: Beyond Aesthetics

The choice of flora within a project does more than beautify; it shapes the environmental and social fabric of the community. By selecting a variety of plants, flowers, and trees, developers can promote biodiversity, improve air quality, and create spaces that encourage community interaction. For instance, the Ghosh family relishes the seasonal blooms and the shade of neem and banyan trees in their community garden, which has become a cherished gathering spot, illustrating how landscaping can foster a sense of belonging and collective well-being.

Ensuring Green Continuity:
The Role of Maintenance

The transition of landscaping care from the developer to a Facility Management (FM) agency is pivotal. A well-documented handover that includes detailed information on plant care, water management, and seasonal gardening activities ensures the longevity and vibrancy of the community's green spaces. The Mukherjee family's experience highlights this transition's success, where the developer's commitment to educating the FM team on the specific landscaping needs preserved the project's green legacy.

Embracing the Green: Questions for the Eco-conscious Homebuyer

To truly understand and appreciate the landscaping efforts in your potential home, consider asking:

➢ Can you describe the landscaping philosophy of the project, including the balance of hardscape and softscape?

➢ What types of plants, flowers, and trees are planned, and how were they selected for this environment?

➢ How does the project plan to maintain these landscaped areas, and what measures are in place for the transition to an FM agency?

➢ What role does landscaping play in the project's overall vision for community well-being and environmental sustainability?

Conclusion

The landscaping of a residential project is a testament to its commitment to creating spaces that nurture the body, mind, and spirit. "Cultivating Serenity" underscores the critical role of thoughtful landscaping in enhancing the quality of life, urging homebuyers to consider this often-overlooked aspect as they search for their dream home. By valuing the integration of green spaces into their living environment, homebuyers can ensure their new home offers not just a place to reside but a sanctuary to flourish.

Chapter-20

The Two Pathways Forward

As we approach the culmination of our journey together through the intricacies of home buying, you might wonder, "Why have I shared the secrets of home buying with such openness?"

One of my mentors once imparted a piece of wisdom that has guided my approach: "Share the most secretive insights generously, which others might guard jealously."

Drawing from countless meetings and interviews, I've endeavored to equip you with knowledge that transforms complexity into clarity. However, as we stand at this juncture, you're presented with two choices:

1st Choice

Armed with the insights shared, you now possess a deeper awareness that sets you apart from the average homebuyer. But remember, what we've explored merely scratches the surface. Questions may still linger, shadows of doubt that could cloud your path. Fear not, for I am here to illuminate the way forward in the chapters that follow.

However, the journey of learning is unending, and the practical experience carries nuances that words can only suggest. Without this firsthand understanding, obstacles may arise, carrying a cost far greater than financial.

2nd Choice

Alternatively, you can choose to have me and my team of home buying experts by your side, ensuring a home buying journey free from stress, guesswork, and unnecessary hurdles.

If you opt for this path, rest assured that an irresistible offer awaits you in the following chapter—an offer designed to simplify your journey to home ownership, making it a voyage of discovery and delight.

Chapter-21

The Enlightened Decision

Congratulations on making the enlightened decision by choosing the path of guidance and support.

I trust this book has been a beacon of knowledge, aiding you in navigating the complex waters of home buying. Yet, the prospect of discussing these insights over a cup of chai or coffee excites me greatly. Hence, I extend to you a special invitation:

Offer 1: A Personal Consultation with me, Yashaswi Shroff, India's 1st home buying scientist with over 100 years of home buying wisdom

Encounter: Spend 15 minutes in a one-on-one session with me, dedicated to demystifying your home buying journey.

Purpose: Gain clarity on any lingering doubts, ensuring your decision is informed, precise, and right the first time.

Offer 2: Continuous Learning through LinkedIn

Engagement: Connect with me on LinkedIn for a continuous stream of home buying tips and secrets.

Benefit: Stay ahead with daily insights, empowering you to make informed decisions every step of the way.

○ ○ ○ ○